T0142528

Like the untouchable wind

An anthology of poems

Edited by Makhosazana Xaba

A Collaboration between
GALA and SRC

Publication © MaThoko's Books
Copyright © Gay and Lesbian Memory in Action (GALA)
© The copyright for each individual poem remains with the poet

First published in 2016 by MaThoko's Books

ISBN: 978-1-928215-47-9

Typesetting and design: Louise Topping

This book was produced with the generous financial support of The Aids Foundation of South Africa and The Other Foundation

MaThoko's Books is an imprint of Gay and Lesbian Memory in Action (GALA).

See a complete list of GALA/MaThoko's Books titles at www.gala.co.za.

Contents

Foreword

Graeme Reid

In 1995 President Robert Mugabe condemned 'gays' in a vitriolic speech delivered at the Zimbabwe International Book Fair, in Harare. Gays and Lesbians of Zimbabwe (GALZ) had a stall at the fair, but were banned by the government from further participation. GALZ's presence signaled increased public visibility, and the president's hostile reaction presaged further state-led attacks on the basic rights of Zimbabwe's lesbian, gay, bisexual, transgender and intersex (LGBTI) communities.

It is no coincidence that this attack took place at a book fair. At stake were the fundamental freedoms of association and expression for Zimbabwe's emerging LGBTI movement. Zimbabwe has since become synonymous with the cynical manipulation of homophobia for political ends. And the chorus of state-sanctioned homophobic rhetoric continues to echo in the region, including in Malawi, Nigeria, Namibia, Tanzania, Uganda and Zambia. More than two decades after the book fair debacle, LGBTI people in Zimbabwe face considerable challenges, including discriminatory laws, arbitrary arrests and homophobic violence that goes unchallenged by the authorities. In these conditions, why turn to poetry?

The anthology, *Like the untouchable wind*, as process and product, evokes the words of Audre Lorde:

"For women then poetry is not a luxury. It is the vital necessity of our existence. It forms the quality of light within which we predicate our hopes and dreams toward survival and change, first made into language, then into idea, then into more tangible action."

The process of writing brought together a group of self-identified lesbians in Bulawayo, Zimbabwe. The starting point for the collection is individual, deeply felt experience. The end result – this anthology – reflects the insights of a community and represents a call to activism: first language, then idea, then tangible action.

Too often lesbian voices are muted or silenced altogether. Lesbians are often spoken for, or misrepresented, demonized, or portrayed as passive victims of discrimination and violence. The authors in this anthology speak for themselves. Khosi Xaba, editor, led the women on a journey in which they shared their experiences, wrote about them, responded to each other's work and then shared them with a wider community.

The poems give a glimpse into the lived experience of lesbians in Zimbabwe: rage, passion, loss, love and lust are all part of a call to action that Sikhulile Sibanda evokes when she refers to her lover as inspiration and 'tool of my activism'.

Silence and invisibility perpetuate the idea that LGBTI people are not part of the social fabric – including the pervasive myth that 'homosexuality is not part of African culture'. By contrast, the poets creatively challenge false assumptions and assert their agency as active participants, creating meaning in their own lives, despite the considerable obstacles that they face.

In her poem 'Tear Gas' (1969), Adrienne Rich wrote:

"I need a language to hear myself with
To see myself in"

The poetry in this anthology is about finding voice, conveying experience and inspiring activism.

Since its inception, GALA has sought to document queer experience, historical and contemporary, to affirm LGBTI experience and counter stereotypes and misconceptions. This project would not have been possible without a strong partnership with the Sexual Rights Centre (SRC), working to promote a sexual rights culture that upholds equality, dignity and respect for all.

Graeme Reid
Founder of GALA and Chair of the Board of Trustees
New York, 29 August 2016

Poetry for Advocacy

Nombulelo Madonko

The Sexual Rights Centre (SRC) conducted a five-day creative writing workshop with GALA, facilitated by Makhosazana Xaba (Khosi), focusing on the lived experiences of queer women in relation to faith and tradition in Zimbabwe. The session was facilitated by Khosi, who is a South African poet and writer, with the assistance of myself, Nombulelo Madonko, a programme officer at the SRC.

When GALA first approached the SRC to collaborate on this writing workshop, we were all too happy to do it as we know that many queer women in Bulawayo are gifted writers and would benefit immensely from the opportunity to refine their skills while also being able to tell their stories in a creative way. This would also tie in perfectly with the work of the SRC, as we conduct fortnightly workshops, called creative spaces, where individuals participate in creative advocacy activities through dance, theatre, music and art. Creative advocacy is an important component of the work of the SRC because not everyone can write or enjoys writing academic documents. It allows people to participate in advocacy, utilising other areas of strength, and richly contributes to the overall goal. The work of the SRC, and specifically the creative advocacy component, is not very common among NGOs in Zimbabwe, although we have seen other organisations take up this work in recent years – possibly based on inspiration from the SRC!

Through consultation with SRC staff members, participants whom they felt would benefit from this experience were hand-picked. Some participants were chosen as they had taken a keen interest in creative advocacy and it was felt that a writing workshop would further widen their experience and develop new avenues of expression. Initially, participants were intimidated when Khosi explained to them what the week would look like as they felt they were not professional writers and would not be able to come up with noteworthy pieces of work. It was amazing to see even the shyest members of the group come out of their shells and gain confidence in their own writing. It gave individuals a self-confidence boost and even those who were initially reluctant to share their work, were soon volunteering to share their work first.

This sort of workshop would definitely be something that the SRC would do again with other community members if the opportunity and funding were available. The individuals who participated in the workshop with Khosi came to the realisation that writing is not reserved for professionals and that we all have an inner skill that we can harness and refine.

Initially when GALA approached the SRC, the idea was to publish the writing of the participants in a local journal. However it was a major challenge to identify a journal in which to publish the work. This is how the idea of this book was born. The SRC and writers alike are very excited to see the final product, in the form of this book, because nothing of this sort has been produced before by the SRC. The SRC intends to share this book with all stakeholders interested in its work and to use it as a tool to inform programming, specifically for queer women. The book speaks directly to the lived experiences of queer women and has allowed the women to speak for themselves in spaces where they cannot be present.

Introduction

Makhosazana Xaba

This volume, *Like the untouchable wind: an anthology of poems*, is a product of the open and creative minds of individuals who participated in a 5-day writing workshop I facilitated during the last week of October 2015. The title of the anthology was suggested by one of Duduzile Salitaire Maseko's poems. Participants opened themselves up to thinking in different ways and brought their creative selves to bear in writing these poems. The writing workshop was a space for women who identify as lesbian to spend time together in a safe environment where we could use writing as a tool for self-expression.

Nombulelo Madonko had told me categorically when we planned the workshop that the participants would like some sessions of the writing workshop to include poetry. As a poet, I was excited. For two of the five days we were all poets: we thought, talked, wrote and read poetry. And every day we began the day with a free writing exercise in order to get us into writing gear.

There is a growing need and realization in the southern African region to record compilations like this one. In 2013 a Cape Town based organisation, Free Gender, put together an anthology of lesbian stories and poems called *Rivers of Life*. The dedication from *Rivers of Life* resonates deeply with the content of this anthology. It resonates with the experiences shared by participants during the workshop in Bulawayo:

"This book is dedicated to all lesbians
Who lost their lives for the sake of love. We
also wish strength to all lesbians who
still live in fear – in their homes and in
their communities....
Finally we also dedicate this book to
everyone who stands up to homophobia
and patriarchy."

Two of the five days were structured to cover the broad theme of using one's voice through poetry to speak out for oneself. The agenda for the two days appears as appendix 1. The exercises I had developed were meant to inspire and focus the writing. At the end of each exercise, we reflected on and discussed how the exercise had worked for each participant; shared lessons, surprises and realizations and then only volunteers read aloud to the group. The emphasis of this process was on allowing each exercise to direct thinking and feelings; to probe memories and project futures. This gives more value to the process rather than the poem or its quality. Participants were not allowed to judge the volunteer reader's poem but were rather invited to comment on *how the poem made them feel* or how they connected to it. Hearing people's emotional response to your poem was valued more than receiving a literary critique of the poem. After all, only two participants - Carol and Pugeni - in the room are also poets in their daily lives. It would therefore not have been reasonable or productive to comment on the literary qualities of poems. We focussed on individual processes – deliberately – in order to surface, for each person, the steps in their journey. Understandably some of the reflections brought back many a painful memory. Participants found very useful the time given to thinking about one's own reflections and, to have others listen and ask clarifying questions.

The poems were as varied as the individuals in the room, a testimony to how unique we all are. While everyone wrote a poem for each exercise, participants were asked to select from those, the ones they wished to publish in this anthology. My task was to work with each submission and suggest, where necessary, the changes that would strengthen the poems – be they structural or editorial.

The anthology opens with Blu's, "Fixation" a playful, erotic poem, which brings a smile to the reader and reminds us about the possibilities of poetry. Humour abounds, yet the serious message also comes through. Similarly in Blu's third poem, "Dear Me, I just became god", the pleasant combination of humour and seriousness seems to suggest this may just be Blu's unique trait. And in, "Living in my future" Blu reminds readers about the power of words: *Words, sentence, phrases and statements/Freeing Mona Lisa, tickling her to laughing frenzies.*

In Sikhulile's poems, the themes of her identity as a visual artist and as a woman and a lesbian speak out loud. Her poems contain affirmation, aspiration, celebration and determination. They paint a picture of who she is, as an award-winning artist and whom she aspires to become as a human being.

Norma handles the universal human themes of love and death as well as activism in her three poems. Portia's meditative poems, "Leaving this behind" and, "Maybe, just maybe" remind us of the constant journey of making choices and decisions, while the rage in Pugeni's poem, "Angry Black Woman" adds texture to these journeys because sometimes, we have to be angry because it does become the most appropriate thing do to. And, we have to do the responsible thing of owning up to it.

Duduzile's poems remind us of the perennial menace of the violent nature of hate crimes. The impact of the violence rings in her poem, "Heartbreak" when she writes *Insomnia has taken a whole new meaning/My life honestly has gone bleak.* Duduzile wrenches readers back to the reality of violence against women and lesbians. I hope that after reading her poem readers will ask themselves the question: "What am I going to do about this problem?" We know that nothing changes until a critical mass of people stands up, speaks up and acts.

The anthology closes with Caroline's poems wherein she takes us to nature via her poems: "Pole, once a tree"; "Battle Bird"; and "Ant". In these poems we are reminded of the nature outside of ourselves. We are invited to look out and engage. As we go through a time when environmental issues become more and more urgent as discussion and activism points because of the impact they have on human beings, these poems tickle the conscience. Caroline's personal poems carry powerful images as well as emotion and are a pleasure to read.

"That throb upon which I am royalty
That powerful almost frightful loyalty
When and where my dreams manifest
When she whoever she may be
Fills me with rhythmic glee"

On the last day of the workshop the Sexual Rights Centre (SRC) staff was invited to listen to the readings. Participants chose one poem to read to the audience and some staff members at SRC also read their own poems.

It is our wish that this volume of 22 poems gives hope to activists who are aspiring writers and those who might be wondering about the value of poetry. There are living examples in our lives already where poetry *has* changed lives, so we all hold onto that hope. Maybe, someone's life will change for better after reading one of these poems.

Blu is a visual story teller who does photography and sometimes dabbles in poetry. She has recently taken to documentary making. Her passion is addressing "the elephant in the room" – the controversial issues society would rather shy away from, particularly the ones involving women and the girl child. While in India she worked on an online campaign, Break the Silence, which saw taboo issues such as menstruation being talked about openly. She also worked on an awareness campaign for Parivathna – a group of disadvantaged women who recycle and reuse paper to make notebooks as well as handbags. At home she has worked with Girl Grandeur, an organisation seeking to uplift women's entrepreneurial, educational and mentorship skills from an early age.

Fixation

I woke up with
Bloodshot eyes, tremors, a dry mouth
Slurred speech, cravings
And, impaired coordination

Itsyour…
Your thighs, your lips
Your calves, your hips
Your hair…did I mention your lips?

Because you're my Fixation
My craving, my bad habit
My compulsion, my Jones
The itch I want not, will not
Cannot scratch
My Fixation!

Itsyour…
Your thighs, your lips
Your calves, your hips
Your hair…Did I mention your lips!

My nicotine, my caffeine
My cannabis, my hashish
The itch I cannot scratch
My Ambrosia
The Quintessence of me

Living in My Future

Voices echoing in my head
Resounding gongs, whispers and tales
Not to be ignored.

Stories, pictures and images worrying me to a frenzy
A frenzy driving me to a revolt
A revolution of words never to be ignored
Tales and whispers, inanimate becomes animated.
Words, sentences, phrases and statements
Free, unfettered
No consequences
Words, sentences, phrases and statements
Moulding modern Athens,
Stirring Shakespeare
Serenading Mozart
Words, sentences, phrases and statements
Freeing Mona Lisa, tickling her to laughing frenzies.

A god of the words inspiring,
Titillating and moulding the present
Emperors, Kings, Queens and street urchins
A god of words birthing new nations
Birthing revolutions
Birthing present futures
A god - of words, phrases, statements and sentences.

Dear Me, I just became god

Brick by brick, brick and mortar and glass
Together they stand, myriad compounds
Marble, sand and metal, clanking together
To bring forth mellifluous sounds of life.
Elements presenting a cacophony of life.

Silence speaking loudly to my limbs
Shaking every nerve in me.
Blood flows like a river. Unfettered life
All but silence. A loud clanking.
The cacophony of life.

House of lizards, peeling rocks,
Athens, this is how you were made.
Dear Me, I just became god.
I claim dominion over all these;
To my glory and for my eyes,

The cacophony clamours on.

Dear Me, I just became god.
Lizards, ants, fruit, flower
All for my use...all to my glory
I stand tall, I can trample all
But I choose not to.

Sikhulile Precious Sibanda is a 44 year-old lesbian, who is a feminist, human rights activist and an award-winning visual artist. The key theme of her art works is observing humanity in its present state. Her works represents a desire to understand communication and the slippage between what is said, what is meant and what is understood. She has participated in numerous visual arts events and festivals internationally, including: Algeria, China, Japan, South Africa, and Nigeria. She has worked with the Sexual Rights Centre (SRC), by facilitating Digital Story Telling (DST) Workshops and Art workshops. She is also one of the founder members of an LBT persons' feminist collective called Voice Of the Voiceless (VOVO) which also uses art to advocate for LBT and Women's Rights.

This is who I am

Made to feel powerless
Level of spiritually is high
No matter what you say
This is who I am

When I met her
Every moment with her I enjoyed
Whatever you want, you can say
This is who I am

Calm inside I feel
Change me, you can try
Fight, you can make me
This is who I am

Myself

Self, listen
Self, it shouldn't be hard
Self, look out more
Self, care more
Get rid of the pain that pains you

Self, focus more than others
Self, you do not deserve the pain you feel
Self, deal with your issues

Passion

Brushes paint on canvas
Create a master piece
Draw it all: The exhibition of my life

Expressing myself through wood, stone and metal
Find words when I visualise
Give me a voice to speak without words
Life, life worth living, love of my life

My way of life: Passion
Reason for living
See everything through you
Censored, taboo, my love is for her
Tool of my activism
I travel all over because of you
Winner of awards.

Loving you is all I can do

Attraction came the moment I saw you
Sexual and emotional, deeper is my attraction
Spiritual and physical is part of my attraction

Cancer in society is what
my love for you is called
"Loving you is all I can do"
Why make the choice
When the choice is not mine to make
The choice of my heart I can't ignore
All I can do is to love you

Like the untouchable wind

Norma Stanley is a human rights defender, feminist, a member of the LGBTI community and strongly believes in gender equality. She is an advocate for women's rights on sex and sexuality and the rights of LGBTI persons. She is a founder member of a self-led LBTI women's collective – Voice of the Voiceless (VOVO) which seeks to ensure the visibility of LBTI women's issues. She loves cooking, movies, reading and being indoors. She is colour blind and not affiliated to any political party but is an activist on feminism. Her favourite fruits are pears, grapes and apples and she loves surprises. She is in a relationship.

In my heart

Oh! Listen to me woman
You are like the sun in the morning
Once again, there is sunshine in my heart

The space of love and care
Has been born in my heart
Something is happening

Oh listen to me woman
What do you think this is?
A miracle, feeling is so good

Woman where were you all this time?
You are the star and light of my heart
Within the walls of my heart

In my heart I have room only for you
You have given me strength
To reach for the skies

Untimely death

I gain strength
I feel hurt
I feel left alone
Blinded by tears
I dreamt of you.

Yet it wasn't you
Shown what would happen
But I did not understand
After a while it became clear
You became ill.

I did not notice
When it became worse
Then you left me
What have I done to deserve this?
Seasons have changed.

Years have passed
The hurt is gone
With memory now I know
This had to happen
To make me strong.

Forward with the movement

Hating has become common
It is unhealthy.

More time spent comparing
Rather than build bridges.

What is stopping us?
There are common issues within

We understand one another's issues
Let us, ourselves be honest.

The universe, a place for the movement
We shall achieve the change we desire.

Portia Rodrigues was born in Bulawayo. Growing up she was close to a friend who was teased for being gay. Tragically he committed suicide and as a result Portia has been an activist since. When she moved to South Africa she continued her friendship with the LGBTI community there. Upon her return to Zimbabwe, she has worked closely with the Sexual Rights Centre as an Activist for LGBTI issues, particularly in creating awareness and acceptance in religious communities. Portia has attended various workshops and functions of the Sexual Rights Centre. She recently took part in Idahot 2016.

Leaving this behind

I tried to drink myself to a stupor
I cannot hang myself with a rope
Another option was to take an overdose of tablets
Did I play God?
What I did was not a crime
I really need to move on
I must leave this behind

Adrenaline Junkie

As I got to the entrance of the club, I straightened my dress
It was a bright red sequinned stretch fabric
It covered all my fake bits, made them look like a nice packet

My red high heels clicked on the floor as I walked in
I knew it was time to begin
I smelt good, my perfume left a trail
I had shoplifted it without a thought of bail
I smelt like I was used to the good life
I smelt like I would make a good wife

I headed straight to the bar, casually tossed my wig
I ordered a whisky and took a swig
Across the bar I caught the stare of a man
I smiled sweetly and thought catch me if you can

I am an adrenaline junkie, there's no stopping me
My heart beating against my chest, betraying me
I beckoned him to come over, chastised myself
I was not prepared to stay on the shelf
Damn it, this won't end well
When he finds out that I am not a girl.

Maybe, just maybe

To move on or not to move on, that is the question
I am set in my ways and enjoy my own company
Do I really want to start all over again
Am I really for the heartache and the pain

What method do I use to choose my next partner
Will gender be an issue?
Should it be a macho man
Making me feel safe and secure
Or should it be a girl who will love me for me
A girl with the softest lips and a big heart
Who will put her arm around me protectively
Daring the world to come near at its own risk.

Should I get a hat, throw in names of suitable candidates
Close my eyes and pick one
After all, life is about taking chances
I mean what's the worst that could happen

The more I think about it
The more stressed I become
Maybe, just maybe I will leave it for another year.

Pugeni was born as Amanda Thandeka Pugeni in the year 1989. She did her primary education at Manondwane in Nketa Bulawayo and Gokomere in Masvingo. Her secondary education was at St James Girls High and Foundation College. She later proceeded to Lupane State University and did an honours degree in Language and Communication. She started doing poetry at a tender age at primary school. Since then she's been writing poetry and performed at various events. She has also written a play and a short story. At present she's working on a script for a short film entitled *Where to from here?*

Angry Black Woman

I am an angry woman
I am the dark shadow you are afraid of
The storm on a sunny day
The cry of the children
The rough edges of a rock
The irritating eyebrow in your eye
The heavy wind disturbing the fields
I am the hurricane
I am not known
This is not poetry its fury!

I am that black angry woman
You are trying to ignore
Beautiful on the outside
Dark on the inside
The emotions raging like a black bull
I am an outcast
The thorn on the rose
The clean water flowing into the sewer
You do not know me
This is not poetry its rage.

Need I say more?
I still feel the nudge to go on
You do not know me
I am the disappointment to the elders
The taboo in the community
The sign for the coming of age
The dirty water in a pothole

I am the angry black woman
The blacken piles of rotten garbage
The broken glass

The threat to the nation
The butterfly trying to get out of the cocoon
The 1000 years of slavery
You know me not.

I am that barking biting dog
The new kid on the block
The hair in your food
The stinking breath
The song of the politicians
The unnoticed hard worker
You know me not.
This is not poetry its rage!

Duduzile Salitaire Maseko was born on 10 of October 1984. She attended Mount Cazalet Primary School and thereafter went to Solusi Adventist and Bulawayo Adventist High Schools. She attended college and graduated with a higher credit in the Advanced Diploma in Computer Science and Information Processing.

Heartbreak

Deep in pain, I'm sinking
Sinking to rise no more
The soul is drained
Pierced by words untimed

Yesterday has become blurred
Tomorrow I do not expect at all
What is life, if you are alone?
The pain that mounts inside
Is conquering the strength of my belief in love

I'm going through turmoil
Losing touch with everything
My world has shattered
Like the wind so untouchable
Like the river, it has flowed

For the first time
Insomnia has taken a whole new meaning
My life honestly has gone bleak
This is then I'm walking down
Life's lonely road.

An Attack

As I approach the corner
So does a gang
I sweat
I wet my pants

The next was laughter and hate speech
Then a blood stained concrete
As clenched fists pounded on my naked skin

Blows raining endlessly
Beaten senseless
Left lying down with no defences

A swollen body
A battered soul
A bleeding heart
A shattered spirit
An attack on my existence.

Caroline Mudzengi is a 25-year-old Zimbabwean bisexual woman. She is a member of a feminist-led collective called Voice of the Voiceless (VOVO), a member of Gays and Lesbian in Zimbabwe (GALZ) and a stakeholder at the Sexual Rights Centre (SRC). She also sits on their LGBTI Advisory Panel. She draws inspiration from female artists such as the late Maya Angelou, who use their talent to fight against injustices. She is a tattoo artist and performing artist, largely doing poetry. She has been an activist since she was a teenager. She participated in a YouTube campaign for marriage equality in Ireland:
https://www.youtube.com/watch?v=XEoMJOwDGEg
https://www.youtube.com/watch?v=YYSmQWg0cC8

Pole, Once a tree

She was ripped from her place
Her beauty unfit for earth's face
Carried to a distant land
After being bashed, gagged and hanged
Heart bled and wept
She screamed but on their mission they hastened
They trimmed, shaped and oiled her

Then as if to spite her they jammed her–
back where they had uprooted her
Where once she lived majestically alive;
She now stands lifeless: motionless, soulless.

Overstood

Standing on a "churu" anthill
As if to chant like Mr. Churchill
Whose word was distilled in conspicuous revision
Of vices, of spices and constant trances
The war being that for being at peace
The calmness infernal, internal, eternal
No matter how bad it is; they do worse before better
The spirit best kept, never lost even to the worst
Mindful nature, mindless misbehavior

Battle bird

She holstered the tiny pistols
Two at a time; just how she got lost the last time.
She tweaked them; felt points, as the bullets got into the chamber.
Ready to fire; hot blazing sharp shooting ambers
So intense a sensation; nothing like what she'd ever felt.

Visions crossed her mind:
an orchestra took her to the edge of the world and back.
The draft in their cocoon seemed to consume the air.
Hours passed as moments of repair
Her broken bones mending and blending with boneless hardenings.
She and Her. Rhythmic, melodious bang

Speak to me

Of chalices and scepters
A place and point where my soul is no longer syphoned
Slowly sapped by the binaries and boxes that I now call home

Of radical inception and conception of an existence
An existence infused with spiritual decay
To a place and point where my other selves can dwell

A meager supply is in surplus of intensity
A soft moan surrendering with the groan
The staffs, rods and poles not wanting my I and I port.
Not feeling the need to replenish my chalice
It is filled; meshed with another, perfect fit.

An intensity that explodes in a pulsation
The war for the chalice; internal peace
A thought with the loudest decibel
Majestic, victorious, triumphant, glorious
Contentment, imprisoned no more
Release: a soft moan.

Ant

She steps in into the shoe print and tyre tread imprint
Pauses a momentous silent pause
In rememberance of both her pre and post fellows

Now I step differently.
I am who I am – nothing can take that away from me.
Who I am cannot be beaten, shouted, insulted, threatened,
raped, coerced or out-so-called loved out of me.

Future Me

A setting with no settings
A milestone after many miles
A polygraphic zone where the time zones are as per setting
Of apparitions on holograms
In a tasteful flavour
Where I need not involuntarily fervor

Where my solitude is my splendor
Where my fiery soul is replenished
When my pivotal summit, begins my adventure
Monotony and monopoly vanquished

That throb upon which I am royalty
That powerful almost frightful loyalty
When and where my dreams manifest
When she whoever she may be
Fills me with rhythmic glee

I say, mean, feel - my love eternal

Agenda of the Poetry Section of the Writing Workshop

DAY 1: MONDAY, 26 OCTOBER 2015
MAIN FOCUS: Poetry and Voice

09:00 – 10:30	Introductions, Expectations & Ground Rules

COMFORT BREAK

10:45 – 12:30	Speaking about poetry in our lives: Sharing Stories

LUNCH

13:30 – 15:00	Exploring urgent issues: The List Poem Exercise

COMFORT BREAK

15:15 – 17:00	Exploring journeys: The Narrative Poem Exercise

DAY 2: TUESDAY, 27 OCTOBER 2015
MAIN FOCUS: Poetry and Narration

09:00 – 10:30	Being in Touch: The Walking and Free Verse Exercise

COMFORT BREAK

10:45 – 12:30	Connecting with others: Talking in Pairs, Inspiring Free Verse Exercise

LUNCH

13:30 – 15:00	Drawing a better future: Exercise

COMFORT BREAK

15:15 – 17:00	Using the drawing above to start a poem

Facilitator Biographies

Nombulelo Madonko is a programmes officer at the Sexual Rights Centre (SRC), passionate about human rights, with a particular bias towards the rights of minority groups. She has been working with the organisation since February 2012. After completing a degree in Social Sciences at the University of Cape Town, she returned to Zimbabwe and volunteered at a youth organisation for a year before joining the SRC. She enjoys working at the SRC because of the creative methods of advocacy that they use, making the work unique and exciting. Nombulelo's work at the SRC has allowed her the privilege to interact with human rights defenders from all over the world and she has been truly inspired to see the passion and drive within these individuals. It is her belief that as individuals it is our mandate to create a better world for future generations even though we may not get to enjoy it ourselves. Her passion comes from this belief.

Makhosazana Xaba is the author of two poetry collections: *these hands* (2005) and, *Tongues of their Mothers* (2008). Her poetry has been anthologized extensively and translated into Italian, Mandarin and Turkish. In 2014 she was nominated for the poetry category of the Mbokodo awards. Her third collection will be published shortly. She is also the author of, *Running and other stories* (2013), which won the SALA Nadine Gordimer Short Story Award in 2014. She is the co-editor of an anthology of short stories, *Queer Africa: New and Collected Fiction* (2013) which won the 26th Lambda Literary Award for the fiction anthology category in 2014. She is currently co-editing the second *Queer Africa* anthology, due out in late 2016. She is working at GALA on several book projects.

About the Organisations

The Sexual Rights Centre (SRC) is a non-profit grassroots organisation based in Bulawayo, Zimbabwe, dedicated to advancing the sexual, legal, social, and cultural rights of marginalized women, children and men. Formed in 2007, the SRC aims to build a sexual rights culture in Zimbabwe by challenging behaviour and attitudes in society, as well as developing programs focused on upholding international recommendations and standards on sexual rights. The organisation targets vulnerable communities and aims to strengthen people through a human rights-based approach premised on the fundamental principles of equality, dignity and respect for all.

Further information and downloadable resources can be found at www.sexualrightscentre.org

The Gay and Lesbian Memory in Action Trust (GALA) is a centre for lesbian, gay, bisexual, transgender and intersex culture and education in Africa. Our mission is, first and foremost to act as a catalyst for the production, preservation and dissemination of knowledge on the history, culture and contemporary experiences of LGBTI people. In recent years GALA has also strengthened its commitment to education and movement building. Through our different areas of work, GALA makes an important contribution to the achievement and development of the human rights of LGBTI people on the continent, and to social justice more broadly.

Further information ad downloadable resources can be found at www.gala.co.za

Printed in the United States
By Bookmasters